GUITAR

4-CHORD
CHRISTMAS

ISBN 978-1-4950-6610-8

7777 W. BLUEMOUND RD. P.O. BOX 13819 MILWAUKEE, WI 53213

Visit Hal Leonard Online at
www.halleonard.com

Angels We Have Heard on High

Traditional French Carol
Translated by James Chadwick

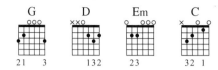

Verse
Moderately

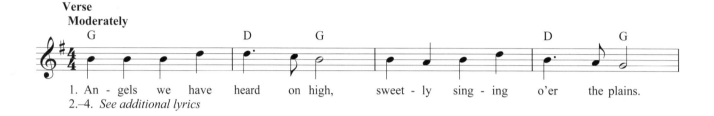

1. An - gels we have heard on high, sweet - ly sing - ing o'er the plains.
2.–4. *See additional lyrics*

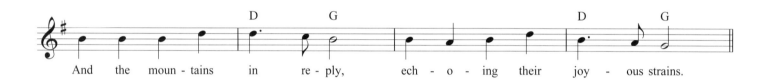

And the moun - tains in re - ply, ech - o - ing their joy - ous strains.

Chorus

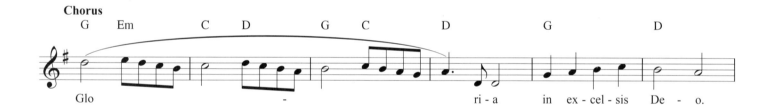

Glo - ri - a in ex - cel - sis De - o.

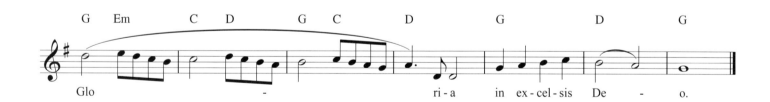

Glo - ri - a in ex - cel - sis De - o.

Additional Lyrics

2. Shepherds, why this jubilee?
   Why your joyous strains prolong?
   What the gladsome tidings be
   Which inspire your heavenly song?

3. Come to Bethlehem and see
   Him whose birth the angels sing.
   Come, adore on bended knee
   Christ the Lord, the newborn King.

4. See within a manger laid
   Jesus, Lord of heaven and earth!
   Mary, Joseph, lend your aid,
   With us sing our Savior's birth.

Bring a Torch, Jeannette, Isabella

17th Century French Provençal Carol

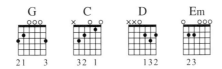

Verse
Brightly

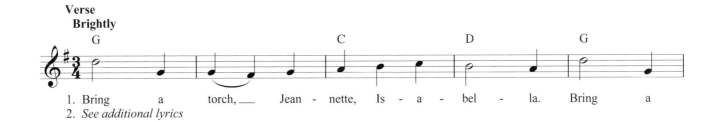

1. Bring a torch, ___ Jean - nette, Is - a - bel - la. Bring a
2. *See additional lyrics*

torch, ___ come swift - ly and run. Christ is born, tell the

folk of the vil - lage, Je - sus is sleep - ing in His cra - dle.

Ah, ah, beau - ti - ful is the moth - er.

Ah, ah, beau - ti - ful is her son. ___

Additional Lyrics

2. Hasten now, good folk of the village,
Hasten now, the Christ Child to see.
You will find him asleep in a manger;
Quietly come and whisper softly.
Hush, hush, peacefully now He slumbers.
Hush, hush, peacefully now He sleeps.

Child of God

Words and Music by Grant Cunningham and Matt Huesmann

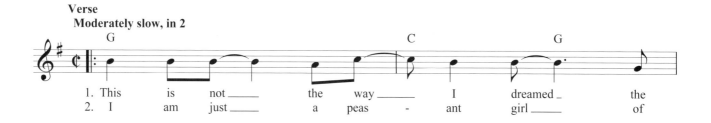

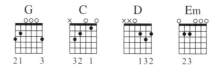

Verse
Moderately slow, in 2

1. This is not ____ the way ____ I dreamed _ the
2. I am just ____ a peas - ant girl ____ of

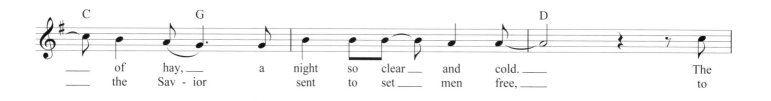

sto - ry would _ un - fold: ____ a sta - ble and ____ a bed _
sim - ple, hon - est means. ____ Who am I ____ to hold _

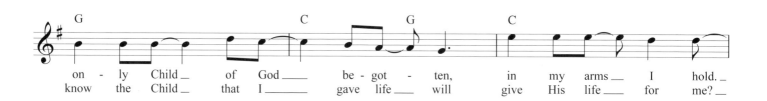

____ of hay, ____ a night so clear ____ and cold. ____ The
____ the Sav - ior sent to set ____ men free, ____ to

on - ly Child _ of God ____ be - got - ten, in my arms ____ I hold. _
know the Child _ that I ____ gave life ____ will give His life ____ for me? _

To us is born _ Em - man - u - el.
The an - gels sing, _ "Em - man - u - el."

Chorus

Ho - ly Child of _____ hope, per - fect Child of _____

peace, born to be _____ the Lord _____ of life _____ in _____

_____ me. _____ Oh, my pre - cious _____ Son, Heav - en's

Child has _____ come to make of me _____ a

child _____ of God. God.

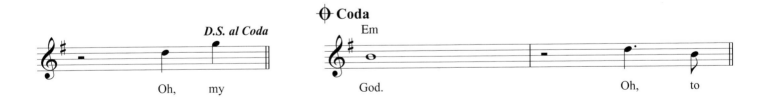

D.S. al Coda

Oh, my

Coda

God. Oh, to

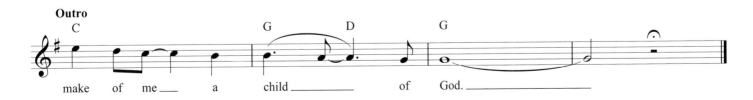

Outro

make of me _____ a child _____ of God. _____

Deck the Hall

Traditional Welsh Carol

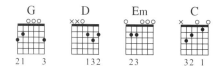

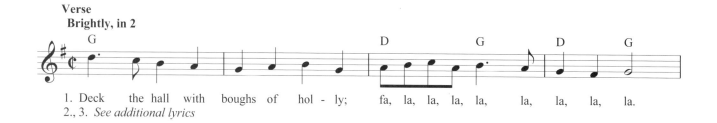

Verse
Brightly, in 2

1. Deck the hall with boughs of hol - ly; fa, la, la, la, la, la, la, la, la.
2., 3. *See additional lyrics*

'Tis the sea - son to be jol - ly; fa, la, la, la, la, la, la, la, la.

Don we now our gay ap - par - el; fa, la, la, la, la, la, la, la, la.

Troll the an - cient yule - tide car - ol; fa, la, la, la, la, la, la, la, la.

Additional Lyrics

2. See the blazing yule before us;
   Fa, la, la, la, la, la, la, la, la.
   Strike the harp and join the chorus;
   Fa, la, la, la, la, la, la, la, la.
   Follow me in merry measure;
   Fa, la, la, la, la, la, la, la, la.
   While I tell of Yuletide treasure;
   Fa, la, la, la, la, la, la, la, la.

3. Fast away the old year passes;
   Fa, la, la, la, la, la, la, la, la.
   Hail the new, ye lads and lasses;
   Fa, la, la, la, la, la, la, la, la.
   Sing we joyous all together;
   Fa, la, la, la, la, la, la, la, la.
   Heedless of the wind and weather;
   Fa, la, la, la, la, la, la, la, la.

Ding Dong! Merrily on High!

French Carol

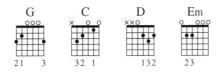

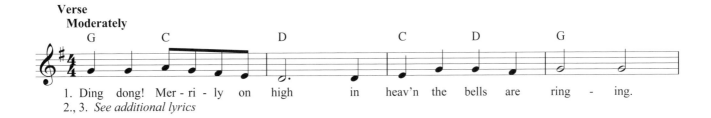

Verse
Moderately

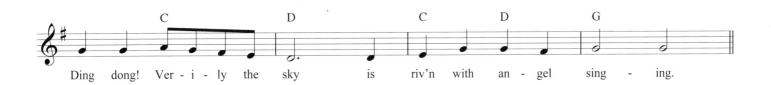

1. Ding dong! Mer - ri - ly on high in heav'n the bells are ring - ing.
2., 3. *See additional lyrics*

Ding dong! Ver - i - ly the sky is riv'n with an - gel sing - ing.

Chorus

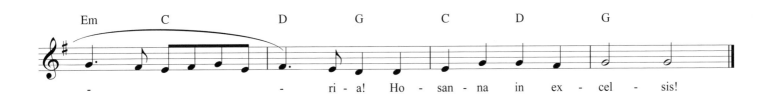

Glo - - - - ri - a! Ho - san - na in ex - cel - sis!

Additional Lyrics

2. E'en so here below, below, let steeple bells be swinging.
   And i-o, i-o, i-o, by priest and people singing.

3. Pray you, dutifully prime your matin chime, ye ringers.
   May you beautiful rime your evetime song, ye singers.

Emmanuel
(Hallowed Manger Ground)

Words and Music by Chris Tomlin and Ed Cash

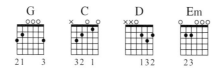

Verse
Reverently, in 2

1. What hope we hold this star-lit night: a King is born in

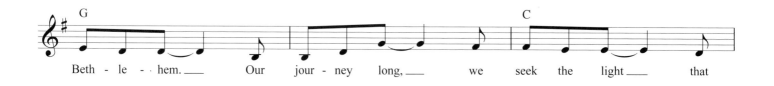

Beth-le-hem. Our jour-ney long, we seek the light that

leads to the hal-low-ed man-ger ground. 2. What

Verse

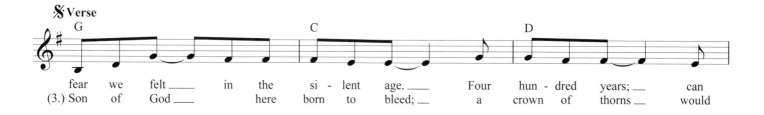

fear we felt in the si-lent age. Four hun-dred years; can
(3.) Son of God here born to bleed; a crown of thorns would

He be found? But bro-ken by a ba-by's cry, re-
pierce His brow. And we be-held this of-fer-ing, ex-

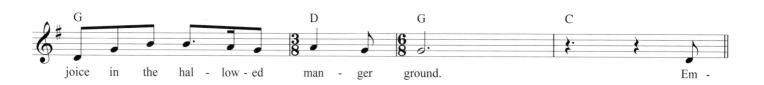

joice in the hal-low-ed man-ger ground. Em-

Feliz Navidad

Music and Lyrics by José Feliciano

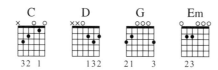

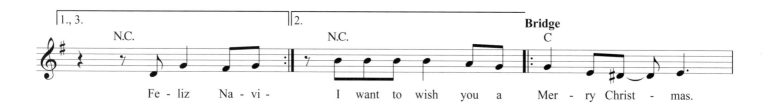

Glad Tidings
(Shalom Chaverim)

English Lyrics and New Music Arranged by Ronnie Gilbert, Lee Hays, Fred Hellerman and Pete Seeger

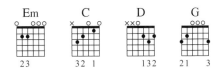

1. Sha - lom cha - ve - rim, sha - lom cha - ve - rim, sha - lom, sha - lom, I'

hit ra - ot, I' hit ra - ot, sha - lom, sha - lom. 2. Glad

tid - ings we bring of peace on earth, good will toward men, of

peace on earth, of peace on earth, good will toward men.

Good King Wenceslas

Words by John M. Neale
Music from *Piae Cantiones*

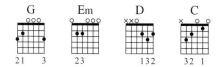

Verse
Moderately

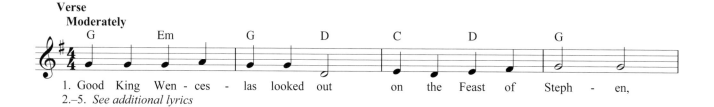

1. Good King Wen - ces - las looked out on the Feast of Steph - en,
2.–5. *See additional lyrics*

when the snow lay 'round a - bout, deep and crisp and e - ven.

Bright - ly shone the moon that night, though the frost was cru - el;

when a poor man came in sight, gath - 'ring win - ter fu - el.

Additional Lyrics

2. "Hither page, and stand by me,
   If thou know'st it telling;
   Yonder peasant, who is he?
   Where and what his dwelling?"
   "Sire, he lives a good league hence,
   Underneath the mountain;
   Right against the forest fence,
   By Saint Agnes' fountain."

3. "Bring me flesh, and bring me wine,
   Bring me pine logs hither;
   Thou and I will see him dine,
   When we bear then thither."
   Page and monarch forth they went,
   Forth they went together;
   Through the rude wind's wild lament,
   And the bitter weather.

4. "Sire, the night is darker now,
   And the wind blows stronger;
   Fails my heart, I know not how.
   I can go no longer."
   "Mark my footsteps, my good page,
   Tread thou in them boldly;
   Thou shalt find the winter's rage
   Freeze thy blood less coldly."

5. In his master's steps he trod,
   Where the snow lay dinted;
   Heat was in the very sod
   Which the saint has printed.
   Therefore, Christian men, be sure,
   Wealth or rank possessing;
   Ye who now will bless the poor,
   Shall yourselves find blessing.

Hark! The Herald Angels Sing

Words by Charles Wesley
Music by Felix Mendelssohn-Bartholdy

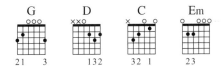

Verse
Joyfully

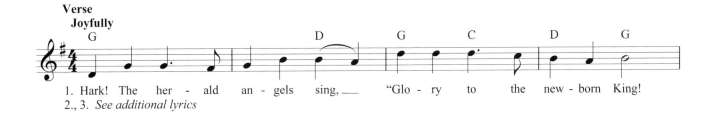

1. Hark! The her - ald an - gels sing, "Glo - ry to the new - born King!
2., 3. *See additional lyrics*

Peace on earth, and mer - cy mild, God and sin - ners re - con - ciled."

Joy - ful all ye na - tions rise. Join the tri - umph of the skies.

With th'an - gel - ic host pro - claim, "Christ is born in Beth - le - hem."

Hark! The her - ald an - gels sing, "Glo - ry to the new - born King!"

Additional Lyrics

2. Christ, by highest heav'n adored,
   Christ, the everlasting Lord;
   Late in time behold Him come,
   Offspring of the Virgin's womb.
   Veil'd in flesh the Godhead see:
   Hail th'Incarnate Deity.
   Pleased as Man with man to dwell,
   Jesus, our Emmanuel!
   Hark! The herald angels sing,
   "Glory to the newborn King!"

3. Hail, the heav'n-born Prince of Peace!
   Hail the Son of Righteousness!
   Light and life to all He brings,
   Ris'n with healing in His wings.
   Mild, He lays his glory by,
   Born that man no more may die;
   Born to raise the sons of earth,
   Born to give them second birth.
   Hark! The herald angels sing,
   "Glory to the newborn King!"

A Holly Jolly Christmas

Music and Lyrics by Johnny Marks

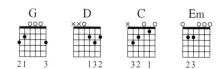

Verse
Moderately bright, in 1

Have a hol - ly jol - ly Christ - mas, it's the best time of the year.

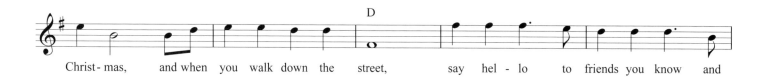

I don't know if there'll be snow, but have a cup of cheer. Have a hol - ly jol - ly

Christ - mas, and when you walk down the street, say hel - lo to friends you know and

ev - 'ry - one you meet. Oh, ho, the mis - tle - toe hung where you can see.

Some - bod - y waits for you, kiss her once for me. Have a hol - ly jol - ly

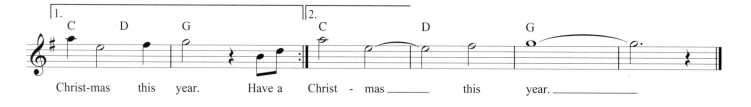

Christ - mas, and in case you did - n't hear, oh, by gol - ly, have a hol - ly jol - ly

Christ - mas this year. Have a Christ - mas this year.

I Heard the Bells on Christmas Day

Words by Henry Wadsworth Longfellow
Music by John Baptiste Calkin

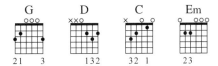

Verse
Moderately slow

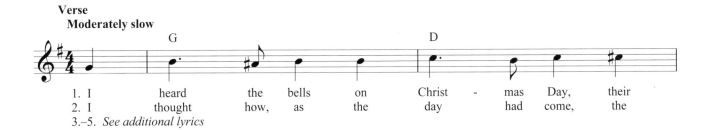

1. I heard the bells on Christ - mas Day, their
2. I thought how, as on the day had come, the
3.–5. *See additional lyrics*

old fa - mil - iar car - ols play. And wild and sweet the
bel - fries of all Christ - en - dom had rolled a - long th'un -

words re - peat of peace on earth, good will to men.
bro - ken song of peace on earth, good will to men.

Additional Lyrics

3. And in despair I bowed my head:
   "There is no peace on earth," I said.
   "For hate is strong, and mocks the song
   Of peace on earth, good will to men."

4. Then pealed the bells more loud and deep:
   "God is not dead, nor doth He sleep.
   The wrong shall fail, the right prevail
   With peace on earth, good will to men."

5. Till, ringing, singing on its way,
   The world revolved from night to day.
   A voice, a chime, a chant sublime,
   Of peace on earth, good will to men.

Infant Holy, Infant Lowly

Traditional Polish Carol
Paraphrased by Edith M.G. Reed

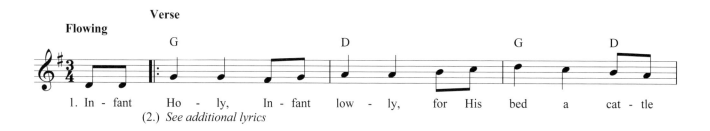

Verse
Flowing

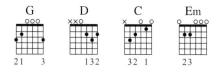

1. In - fant Ho - ly, In - fant low - ly, for His bed a cat - tle
(2.) *See additional lyrics*

stall. Ox - en low - ing, lit - tle know - ing Christ the Babe is Lord of

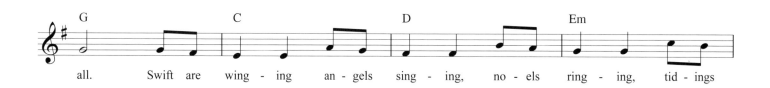

all. Swift are wing - ing an - gels sing - ing, no - els ring - ing, tid - ings

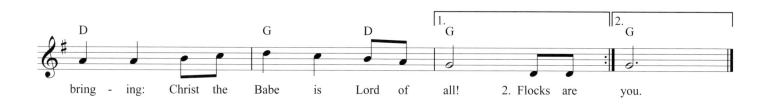

bring - ing: Christ the Babe is Lord of all! 2. Flocks are you.

Additional Lyrics

2. Flocks are sleeping, shepherds keeping
   Vigil 'til the morning new.
   Saw the glory, heard the story,
   Tidings of a Gospel true.
   Thus rejoicing, free from sorrow,
   Praises voicing, greet the morrow.
   Christ the Babe was born for you.

Jolly Old St. Nicholas

Traditional 19th Century American Carol

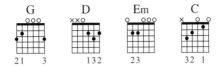

Additional Lyrics

2. When the clock is striking twelve, when I'm fast asleep,
Down the chimney broad and black, with your pack you'll creep.
All the stockings you will find hanging in a row.
Mine will be the shortest one; you'll be sure to know.

3. Johnny wants a pair of skates, Susy wants a sled.
Nellie wants a picture book: yellow, blue and red.
Now I think I'll leave to you what to give the rest.
Choose for me, dear Santa Claus; you will know the best.

Merry Christmas from the Family

Words and Music by Robert Earl Keen

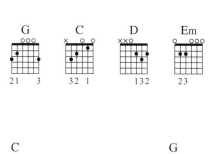

Verse
Moderately

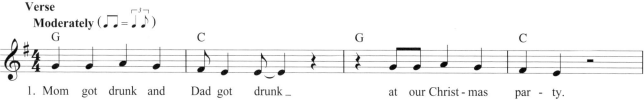

1. Mom got drunk and Dad got drunk at our Christ-mas par-ty.

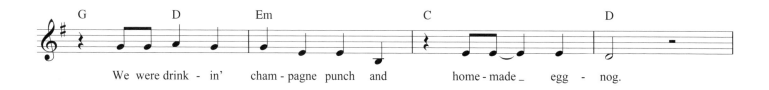

We were drink-in' cham-pagne punch and home-made egg-nog.

Lit-tle sis-ter brought her new boy-friend. He was a Mex-i-can.

We did-n't know what to think of him till he sang, "Fe-liz Na-vi-dad, Fe-liz Na-vi-

dad."

Verse

2. Broth-er Ken brought his kids with him,
3. *See additional lyrics*

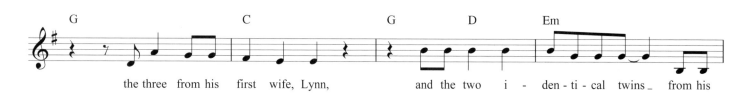

the three from his first wife, Lynn, and the two i-den-ti-cal twins from his

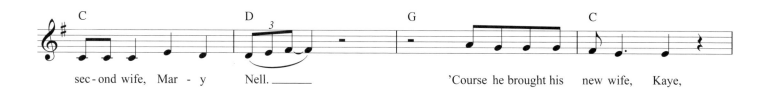

sec-ond wife, Mar-y Nell. 'Course he brought his new wife, Kaye,

Additional Lyrics

3. Fran and Rita drove from Harlingen; I can't remember how I'm kin to them.
But when they tried to plug their motor home in, they blew our Christmas lights.
Cousin David knew just what went wrong, so we all waited out on our front lawn.
He threw the breaker and the lights came on and we sang, "Silent night, oh, silent night."

Mistletoe

Words and Music by Justin Bieber, Nasri Atweh and Adam Messinger

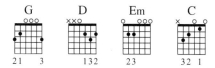

Verse
Easy Reggae feel, in 2

1. It's the most beau-ti-ful time of the year; ___ lights fill the
2. Ev-'ry-one's gath-er-ing a-round the fire; ___ chest-nuts

streets, spread-ing so much cheer. ___ I should be play-ing in the win-ter snow, _
roast-ing like a hot Ju-ly. ___ I should be chill-in' with my folks, I know, _

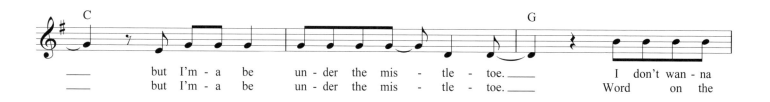

___ but I'm-a be un-der the mis-tle-toe. ___ I don't wan-na
___ but I'm-a be un-der the mis-tle-toe. ___ Word on the

miss out on the hol-i-day, ___ but I can't stop star-ing at your face. _
street: San-ta's com-ing to-night, ___ rein-deers fly-ing through the sky so high. _

I should be play - ing in the win - ter snow, ___
I should be mak - ing a list, ___ I know, ___

but I'm - a be

Chorus

un - der the mis - tle - toe ___ with you, ___ shaw - ty, with you, ___

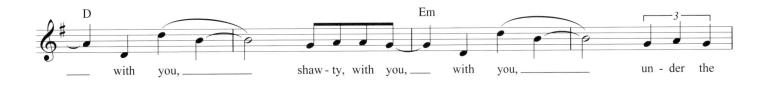

___ with you, ___ shaw - ty, with you, ___ with you, ___ un - der the

1. 2. **Outro**

mis - tle - toe. ___ Kiss me un - der-neath the

mis - tle - toe. ___ Show me, ba - by, that you love me so, oh oh, ___

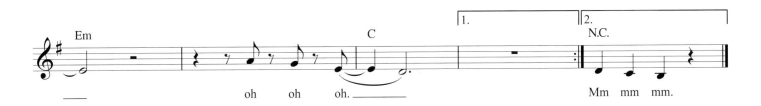

1. 2.

oh oh oh. ___ Mm mm mm.

Not That Far from Bethlehem

Words and Music by Jeff Borders, Gayla Borders and Lowell Alexander

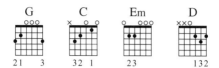

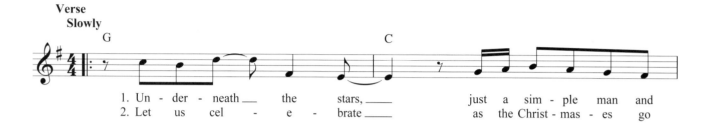

1. Un - der - neath ___ the stars, ___ just a sim - ple man and
2. Let us cel - e - brate ___ as the Christ - mas - es go

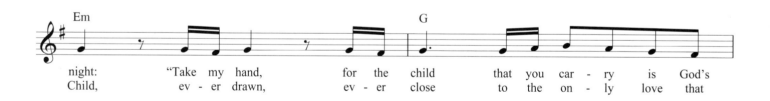

wife. Some - where in ___ the dark, ___ his words cut the si - lent
by, learn to live ___ our days ___ with our hearts near to the

night: "Take my hand, for the child that you car - ry is God's
Child, ev - er drawn, ev - er close to the on - ly love that

own. ___ And though it seems the ___ road is long, ___ we're
lasts. ___ And though two thou - sand ___ years have passed, _ we're

Chorus

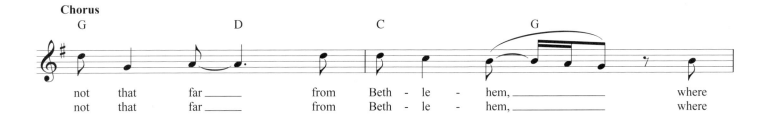

not that far _____ from Beth - le - hem, _____ where
not that far _____ from Beth - le - hem, _____ where

all our hope ___ and joy be - gin. ___ For ___ in our arms, ___ we'll
all our hope ___ and joy be - gin. ___ For ___ when our hearts ___ still

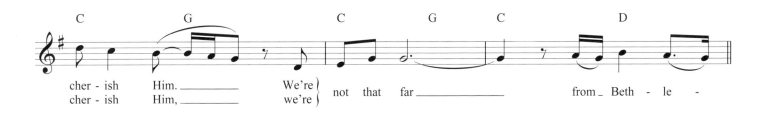

cher - ish Him. _____ We're ⎱ not that far _____ from _ Beth - le -
cher - ish Him, _____ we're ⎰ not that far _____ from _ Beth - le -

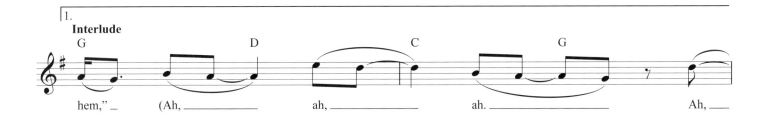

1.
Interlude

hem," _ (Ah, _____ ah, _____ ah. _____ Ah, ___

2.

_____ ah.) _____ from _ Beth - le -   hem. _____

25

Nuttin' for Christmas

Words and Music by Sid Tepper and Roy C. Bennett

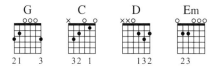

Verse
Brightly, in 2

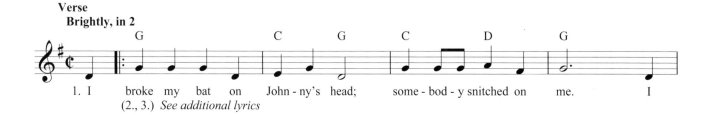

1. I broke my bat on John-ny's head; some-bod-y snitched on me. I
(2., 3.) *See additional lyrics*

hid a frog in sis-ter's bed; some-bod-y snitched on me. I spilled some ink on

Mom-my's rug, I made Tom-my eat a bug, bought some gum with a pen-ny slug;

Chorus

some-bod-y snitched on me. Oh, I'm get-tin' nut-tin' for Christ-mas.

Mom - my and Dad - dy are mad.

I'm get - tin' nut - tin' for Christ - mas, 'cause I ain't been

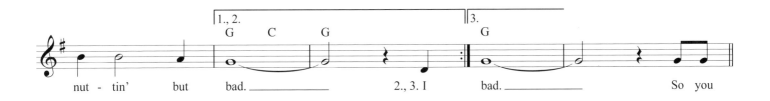

1., 2.

3.

nut - tin' but bad. _____ 2., 3. I bad. _____ So you

Outro

bet - ter be good, what - ev - er you do, 'cause if you're bad, I'm warn - ing you:

you'll get nut - tin' for Christ - mas. _____

Additional Lyrics

2. I put a tack on teacher's chair;
   Somebody snitched on me.
   I tied a knot in Susie's hair;
   Somebody snitched on me.
   I did a dance on Mommy's plants,
   Climbed a tree and tore my pants.
   Filled the sugar bowl with ants;
   Somebody snitched on me.

3. I won't be seeing Santa Claus;
   Somebody snitched on me.
   He won't come visit me because
   Somebody snitched on me.
   Next year, I'll be going straight.
   Next year, I'll be good, just wait.
   I'd start now, but it's too late;
   Somebody snitched on me.

O Come, O Come, Emmanuel

Traditional Latin Text
15th Century French Melody

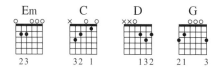

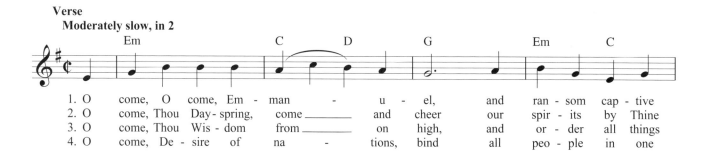

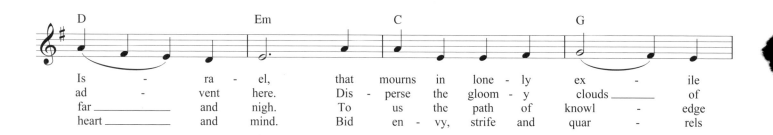

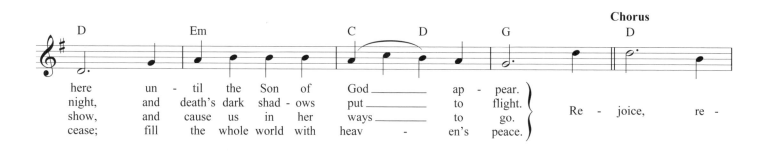

Still, Still, Still

Salzburg Melody, c.1819
Traditional Austrian Text

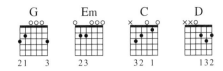

Verse
Moderately slow

1. Still, _____ still, _____ still, to _____ sleep is _____ now His _____
2. Sleep, _____ sleep, _____ sleep, while _____ we Thy _____ vig - il _____

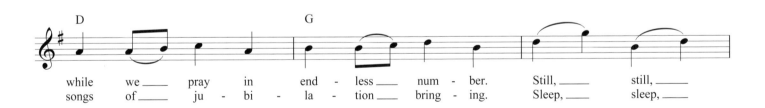

will. On Mar - y's _____ breast He rests in _____ slum - ber,
keep. And an - gels _____ come He from heav - en _____ sing - ing,

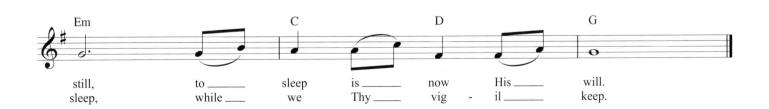

while we _____ pray in end - less _____ num - ber. Still, _____ still, _____
songs of _____ ju - bi - la - tion _____ bring - ing. Sleep, _____ sleep, _____

still, to _____ sleep is _____ now His _____ will.
sleep, while _____ we Thy _____ vig - il _____ keep.

Old Toy Trains

Words and Music by Roger Miller

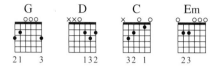

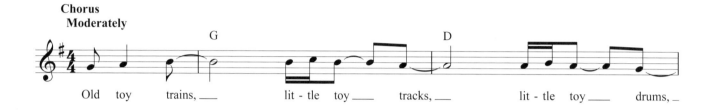

Chorus
Moderately

Old toy trains, ___ lit - tle toy ___ tracks, ___ lit - tle toy ___ drums, ___

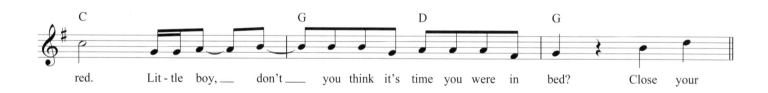

___ com - in' from a sack, car - ried by a man dressed in white and

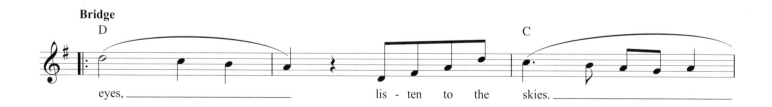

red. Lit - tle boy, ___ don't ___ you think it's time you were in bed? Close your

Bridge

eyes, _____ lis - ten to the skies. _____

All is calm, all is well; soon you'll hear Kris

Krin-gle and the jin - gle ___ bell bring-in' lit-tle toy ___ trains, ___ lit-tle toy ___ tracks, ___

Chorus

___ lit-tle toy ___ drums ___ com - in' from a sack, car - ried by a

man dressed in white and red. Lit - tle boy, ___ don't ___ you think it's time you were in

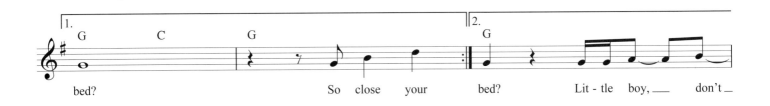

bed? So close your bed? Lit - tle boy, ___ don't ___

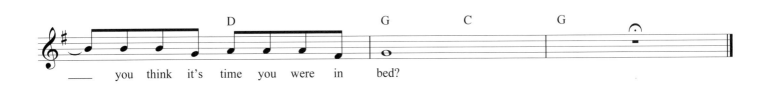

___ you think it's time you were in bed?

Up on the Housetop

Words and Music by B.R. Hanby

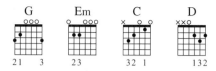

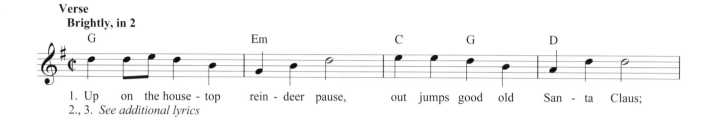

Verse
Brightly, in 2

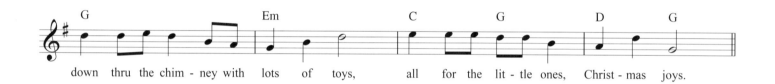

1. Up on the house - top rein - deer pause, out jumps good old San - ta Claus;
2., 3. *See additional lyrics*

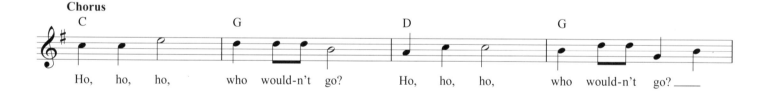

down thru the chim - ney with lots of toys, all for the lit - tle ones, Christ - mas joys.

Chorus

Ho, ho, ho, who would-n't go? Ho, ho, ho, who would-n't go? ____

Up on the house - top, click, click, click. Down through the chim - ney with good Saint Nick.

Additional Lyrics

2. First comes the stocking of Little Nell.
Oh, dear Santa, fill it well.
Give her a dollie that laughs and cries,
One that will open and shut her eyes.

3. Next comes the stocking of little Will.
Oh, just see what a glorious fill!
Here is a hammer and lots of tacks,
Also a ball and a whip that cracks.